# Ruby Bridges

T0002465

## CHERRY LAKE PRESS

Published in the United States of America by Cherry Lake Publishing Group
Ann Arbor, Michigan
www.cherrylakepublishing.com

Reading Adviser: Beth Walker Gambro, MS, Ed., Reading Consultant, Yorkville, IL
Book Designer: Jennifer Wahi
Illustrator: Jeff Bane

Photo Credits: page 5: © Joseph Sohm/Shutterstock; page 7: © Drazen Zigic/Shutterstock; page 9: © Kevin Ruck/Shutterstock; page 11: Library of Congress, Serial and Government Publications Division; page 13: © Vixit/Shutterstock; page 15: © AP Photo; pages 17, 22: © William A. Morgan/Shutterstock; pages 19, 23: © Everett Collection Inc/Alamy Stock Photo; page 21: © Sipa USA/Alamy Stock Photo

**Cherry Lake Press** is an imprint of Cherry Lake Publishing Group.

Library of Congress Cataloging-in-Publication Data

Names: Wing, Kelisa, author. | Bane, Jeff, 1957- illustrator.
Title: Ruby Bridges / written by Kelisa Wing ; illustrated by Jeff Bane.
Description: Ann Arbor, Michigan : Cherry Lake Publishing, 2023. | Series: My itty-bitty bio | Audience: Grades K-1 | Summary: "This biography for early readers examines the life of Ruby Bridges, the first African American student to integrate a school, in a simple, age-appropriate way that helps young readers develop word recognition and reading skills. Includes table of contents, author biography, timeline, glossary, index, and other informative backmatter."-- Provided by publisher.
Identifiers: LCCN 2022043046 | ISBN 9781668919156 (hardcover) | ISBN 9781668920176 (paperback) | ISBN 9781668921500 (ebook) | ISBN 9781668922835 (pdf)
Subjects: LCSH: Bridges, Ruby--Juvenile literature. | African American children--Louisiana--New Orleans--Biography--Juvenile literature. | African Americans--Louisiana--New Orleans--Biography--Juvenile literature. | New Orleans (La.)--Race relations--Juvenile literature. | School integration--Louisiana--New Orleans--Juvenile literature.
Classification: LCC F379.N553 B759 2023 | DDC 379.2/63092 [B]--dc23/eng/20220913
LC record available at https://lccn.loc.gov/2022043046

Printed in the United States of America
Corporate Graphics

**About the author:** Kelisa Wing loves spending time with her family and loves helping others. She lives in northern Virginia.

**About the illustrator:** Jeff Bane and his two business partners own a studio along the American River in Folsom, California, home of the 1849 Gold Rush. When Jeff's not sketching or illustrating for clients, he's either swimming or kayaking in the river to relax.

I was born in 1954 in Mississippi. This was the same year racial **segregation** ended in public schools.

I had four **siblings**. I was the oldest.

How would you describe your family?

We moved to New Orleans when I was 4. This city is in Louisiana.

I was still not allowed to attend certain schools. This wasn't fair.

What else do you think isn't fair?

I was smart. I took a test and passed. I could go to school with all children.

Going to school wasn't safe. I was Black and going to school with White students. People were angry about this. **Federal marshals** walked me to school every day.

I was in a classroom all by myself. I ate lunch alone. But I never missed a day of school.

I was brave. I **inspired**. Later I wrote books about my experience. I won a book award for this.

What change do you want to make in the world?

I helped create change when I was young. And I still work to create change now.

What would you like to ask me?

1960

1940

Born
1954

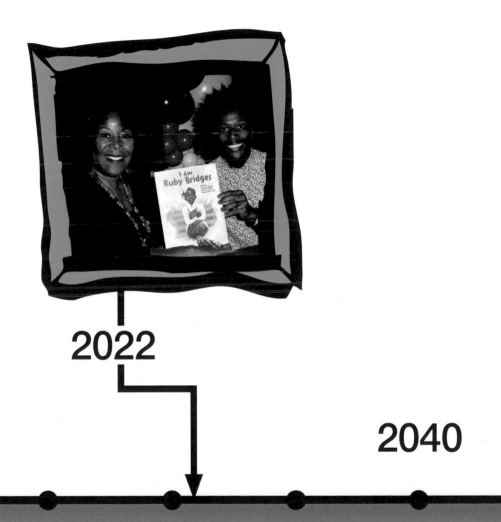

2022

2040

## glossary

**federal marshals** (FEH-duh-ruhl MAR-shuhlz) law enforcement officers who work for federal courts

**inspired (**in-SPYRD) filled someone with a feeling or an idea

**segregation** (seh-grih-GAY-shuhn) separating people based on race

**siblings** (SIH-blings) brothers and sisters

## index